The Little Secret That Can Change Your Life*

The Little Secret That Can Change Your Life*

*If You Win the Rat Race, You're Still a Rat

JOANN DAVIS

CONARI PRESS

First published in 2005 by Conari Press,
an imprint of Red Wheel/Weiser, LLC, York Beach, ME
With offices at:
368 Congress Street, Boston, MA 02210
www.redwheelweiser.com

Library of Congress Cataloging-in-Publication Data
Davis, Joann
  The little secret that can change your life : if you win the rat race, you're still a rat / Joann
Davis.
    p. cm.
  Includes bibliographical references.
  ISBN 1-57324-255-1 (alk. paper)
1. Conduct of life. I. Title.
  BJ1581.2.D3678 2005
  170'.44–dc22

                    2004027518

Photograph on page 61 courtesy of Free-Stock-Photos.com.
Typeset in Baskerville and GillSans by Jill Feron, FeronDesign

Printed in USA
RRD

12 11 10 09 08 07 06 05
 8 7 6 5 4 3 2 1

The paper used in this publication meets the minimum requirements of the American National
Standard for Information Sciences–Permanence of Paper for Printed Library Materials Z39.48-
1992 (R1997).

*For Jenny and Colin who gave me that
"glimpse of truth" for which I had forgotten to ask.*

Contents

Acknowledgments

Allowing that all the errors in this book are mine alone, I wish to thank the following people for their help, love, support, and inspiration.

Joyce Waldon, Michelle Shinseki, Linda Watson, Richard Cohen, Kathyrn Adams Shapiro, Ron Shapiro, Alexis Siroc, Candace Fuhrman, David Black, Liv Blumer, Linda Loewenthal, Susan Raihofer, Jason Barusch, and the one and only Albert—my heartfelt appreciation to all of you, my friends and colleagues.

To Lily Tomlin, who once told *Forbes* that "The trouble with the rat race is that even if you win, you're still a rat."

To Jan Johnson, who took the time, asked the questions, listened, and believed.

To Amy Edelstein for a wonderful editing job.

To Kate Hartke and all the staff of Conari for your dedication.

To my parents, Ann and Paul, and to my sisters, Ellen, Paula, and Donna, who taught me the secret of loving-kindness.

To my children, Jenny and Colin, who each day, without knowing, offer that glimpse of truth for which I had forgotten to ask. My love for both of you is boundless.

And, finally, to Kenny, for whom there are no words—only the steady beating of my heart.

The task which I am trying to achieve is, by the power of the written word, to make you see. That—and no more. And it is everything. If I succeed you shall find there, according to your desserts, encouragement, consolation, fear, charm—all you demand—and perhaps also that glimpse of truth for which you have forgotten to ask.

—FROM *THE NIGGER OF THE "NARCISSUS"* BY
JOSEPH CONRAD

It is from numberless diverse acts of courage and belief that human history is shaped. Each time a man stands up for an ideal, or acts to improve the lot of others, or strikes out against injustice, he sends forth a tiny ripple of hope, and crossing each other from a million different centers of energy and daring, those ripples can sweep down the mightiest walls of repression and resistance.

Like it or not, we live in interesting times, and everyone here will ultimately be judged, will ultimately judge himself, on the efforts he has contributed to building a new world society and the extent to which his ideals and goals have shaped that effect.

—FROM THE "DAY OF AFFIRMATION" SPEECH GIVEN BY ROBERT F. KENNEDY ON JUNE 6, 1966

Winning the Rat Race

A simple woman from humble Irish roots, my mother never went to college. But when I was growing up, she seemed to have all the answers. For instance, if my favorite blouse got a stain on it, she could remove the spot in no time flat with a dab of seltzer. One C in my spelling class quickly became a B+ under her tutelage. And when I wanted to learn how to get the top of the custard to turn golden brown, she taught me the trick of brushing it with butter.

Why, she even had views on philosophy. One time, when I asked how a person could live a happy and meaningful life, her answer was swift.

"Always remember this little secret," she said. "'If you win the rat race, you're still a rat.'"

Years later that piece of advice came back to me when I had children of my own. Like any parent, I wanted my daughter and son to be prepared for the modern world, which can be a pretty hairy place. Let's face it, the world chews people up and crushes their dreams, declaring "nice guys finish last" and "the end justifies the means." Everybody knows "the world loves a winner" and "it's okay to win at any cost"—as long as you win. Kind people are quickly labeled "suckers" if they fall for "it"—whatever "it" is. And, having trained our children to expect rewards for doing what is expected, the world is full of children who grow up to be adults who ask, "What's in it for me?"

The answer to that is very little in terms of true and lasting rewards. We need to make a dramatic change in course. But how do we chart this new course? Where do we begin? For starters, let's agree that, for many of us, life is a rat race. The frantic competition of the world involves running hard just to stay in place on the treadmill of buying and spending; working excessive hours to make ends meet; collapsing each night from exhaustion—mental and physical—only to get up and repeat the same vicious cycle again the next day. Debt, stress, and frustration build up. Precious emotional resources are squandered. Our families are relegated to the "second shift." And like rats in a maze, we wind up in blind alleys with no way out.

The road to this hell is paved with faulty assumptions. For one thing, we see life in material terms, accepting the empty promise of advertisers and marketers that the best things in life are . . . things. We buy into the notion that happiness is for sale if only we find the right store. And we take pride in living a life of "conspicuous industriousness" that confuses being busy with being contented.

Most importantly, we forget an eternal truth: it's possible to gain the world and lose our souls. As Albert Schweitzer once observed, "A civilization which develops only on its material side, and not in corresponding measure in the sphere of the spirit, is like a ship with defective steering gear which gets out of control at a constantly accelerating pace, and thereby heads for catastrophe."

For many people, the catastrophe has arrived. The soaring sales of sleeping pills, antidepressants, and other stress relievers reveal the titanic cost of running the rat race. In an article called, "Matters Have Gotten Out of Hand," Saul Bellow noted, "It's as though people were to say, 'I get home dog tired after a terrible day out in that jungle, and then I don't want to think about it. Enough! I want to be brainwashed. I'm going to have my dinner and drink some beer, and I'm going to sit watching TV until I pass out—because that's how I feel.' That means people are not putting up a struggle for the human part of themselves."

Is this the life we want to live? An existence that threatens to destroy the human part of ourselves?

This little book you hold in your hands says, "No." It suggests that there is a better, richer, and more fulfilling way of life than the rat race. A way that shuns money worship, cutthroat competition, hyper commercialism, and material excess. A way that calls upon each of us to slow down, rearrange our priorities, and put love, caring, and kindness above the empty pursuits of buying, spending, and acquiring. It guides us to banish the "reward mentality" and make virtue its own reward. It inspires us to be captains of our souls rather than slaves of convention; to embrace a more idealistic vision of sacrifice and service as we move from the "me generation" to the "we generation"; to balance our material and spiritual selves; and to value inner worth over outward appearances.

Don't believe it can be done? Then read on and see what might be possible.

Part One, with its bite-sized essays, looks at the "way of the world" or how we live our lives in a highly materialistic, dog-eat-dog fashion. It explores the "Rules for Rats" that govern life in the rat race and examines our society's inclination to define progress only in dollars-and-cents terms and forgets our human needs and inner development. We will look at the subversive role shopping can play in our lives. We will probe why it is that "with the eating comes the appetite." And we will attempt to understand why humans need things that the rat race can't provide.

In Part Two, we will extol a different code of conduct, one that honors virtue as its own reward. We will look at the need to be optimistic and to dream big; to embrace a more idealistic and community-minded outlook that honors those who for too long have been left behind.

In Part Three, we will look at spiritual habits and practices that can take us to a new place; habits such as forgiveness and love that reduce the amount of hate in our world. Because when all is said and done, hate is the greatest weapon of mass destruction in our world today.

And finally, in Part Four, you are invited to take the first step towards creating a life that counts. You can use the space provided to make a personal "Declaration of Enough" in areas of your life where change is needed. You are also invited to make an "ethical will" that identifies the non-material legacy you want to leave your heirs. And in "Five Questions Worth Asking," you are invited to ponder some of life's pressing issues as you chart your new course.

❖

The great nineteenth-century transcendentalist Ralph Waldo Emerson wrote, "As long as our civilization is essentially one of property, of fences, of exclusiveness, it will be mocked by delusions. Our riches will leave us sick; there will be bitterness in our laughter; and our wine will burn our mouth. Only that good profits, which we can taste with all doors open, and which serves all men."

The early twentieth-century theologian and scholar Rabbi Abraham Joshua Heschel once observed, "The problem is the spirit of our age: denial of transcendence, the vapidity of values, emptiness in the heart, the decreased sensitivity to the imponderable quality of the spirit, the collapse of communication between the realm of tradition and the inner world of the individual."

Our inner world is ours to make of what we choose. Magnificent changes can radiate out of every human heart if we so desire. So, then, if you are open, brave, and willing to take up this challenge, read on. See if you don't agree that Mom was right. There is a little secret that can change your life.

Part I
Living in a Dog-Eat-Dog World

Questioning the "Way of the World"

Shh! Someone is describing the "Way of the World." Let's be quiet and listen . . .

Winning isn't everything—it's the only thing.
Swim with the sharks, but don't get eaten alive.
Sue the bastards!
Look out for #1.
Let's scare the pants off them.
Try winning through intimidation.
Go for the jugular.
Nice guys finish last.
To the victors belong the spoils.
We'll teach them a lesson they'll never forget.

No good deed goes unpunished.
Fight fire with fire.
Take no prisoners.
It's all about the Benjamins.
Show me the money.
Only a sucker would fall for that.

The world is a dog-eat-dog place. Does it have to be?

Rules for Rats

Picture yourself in the halcyon days of childhood. You are putting on your jacket, getting ready to leave home, when your mother calls out your name.

"Where are you going?" she asks.

"Out," you say.

"With whom?" she continues.

"My friends," you answer.

"To do what?" she inquires.

"Nothing," you say.

And it was true. You had nothing in mind. Perhaps you would meet a friend, sit on a stoop, stand on a corner, or toss a ball. In the good old days, when the world was a simpler place, children didn't plot and plan. They simply went out and played with kids they liked.

Times have changed. Today, children learn that planning is the hallmark of a well-lived life. They see their parents armed with calendars and date books, making back-to-back appointments and jetting around the country on marathon business trips, seldom stopping to take a breather. The emphasis on being busy is so great that Richard Stengel wrote the following in *The New Yorker:*

> Nowadays, people don't ask you how you are, they say, 'Are you busy?' meaning, 'Are you *well?*' If someone actually does ask you how you are, the most cheerful answer, of course, is a robust 'Busy!' to which the person will reply 'Good!' 'Busy' used to be a negative sort of word. It meant having no time for yourself, no leisure. 'No, I can't come out this

weekend, I'm too busy.' Sorry about that, you poor stiff. Now, though, busyness is bullish. Conspicuous industriousness is the rule.

"Conspicuous industriousness" is fancy talk for chasing your own tail. This is the habit of rushing around frantically and feeling quite noble even when you go nowhere fast. Equipped with cell phones, beepers, and handheld computers, the "conspicuously industrious" blur the line between home and office by working anytime, anywhere. Always on call, they make a perverse case for the argument that work isn't a part of life, but rather that life is a part of work. They embody the new twenty-first century ideal–"I work, therefore I am."

And whether they know it or not, they are competitors in the rat race. Constantly busy, moving at breakneck speed, they wake, work, earn, spend, shovel down food, and collapse—only to begin the same vicious cycle over again the next day. Never knowing which end is up, they live according to the "Rules of the Rat Race," an unwritten code of conduct that says you should:

1. Bite off more than you can chew.
2. Act as if enough is never enough.
3. Chase your tail and run to stand still.
4. View life as a part of work, instead of work as a part of life.
5. Acknowledge that some rats are more equal than others.

Perhaps it was in the aftermath of World War II that the Rules of the Rat Race first took shape. Fresh from victory on the international front, America was basking in a new spirit of optimism and economic prosperity. As cars rolled off the assembly line and houses rose up from the ground in manicured suburbs, there was a feeling of unlimited possibility in the air. The Great Depression was a thing of the past; the standard of living was rising; and scientific innovation was bringing forth everything from the polio vaccine and penicillin to filtered cigarettes and baby formulas.

Promoting these products required special skills. As Jim Wallis reports in *The Soul of Politics,* advertising agencies were ready to do the job, even if it meant stretching the truth. "Advertising is the false spirituality of materialism, promising what it can never deliver," Wallis writes. "Even the slogans of advertising sound religious, using the language of ultimate concern: 'Buick: Something to Believe In'; 'Miller Beer: It Doesn't Get Any Better Than This'; 'G.E.: We Bring Good Things to Life.' Television images of young, beautiful, sexy, successful people enjoying the best of life surround almost every product, and you can be just like them, suggest the ads. If you drink this beer, use this toothpaste, drive this car, wear this perfume, or buy these jeans, this can be your life, too." And as Wallis concludes: "Is this not the essence of idolatry—a misdirected form of worship?"

This misdirected worship was accompanied by a rise in conformity. The need to fit in, to be like everyone else, helped produce a generation of briefcase men who rode the commuter train from the suburbs to the city each morning in a standard uniform of dark suit, white shirt, and tie. Were they happy? They certainly had the veneer of success: houses, picture-perfect families, and lots of discretionary income. So what if they worked too many hours and traveled long distances from home to work? So what if they drank at the end of the day to bury their sorrows? They were living the American Dream. They ran the rat race and seemed to be winning!

Our cultural desire for affluence was nurtured by the media, which also sowed the seeds of discontent. As Barbara Ehrenreich notes in her book, *Fear of Falling: The Inner Life of the Middle Class,* television brought "the most decrepit ghetto dwelling intimate glimpses into the 'lifestyles of the rich and famous,' not to mention the merely affluent. Studying the televised array of products and comforts available, seemingly, to everyone else, the poor become more dangerous."

The gnawing dissatisfaction that was bred helped contribute to a constant drive for economic growth. Not everyone viewed it as a good thing. Former Czech president Vaclav Havel has written that in America "there is the blind worship of perpetual economic growth and consumption, regardless of their destructive impact on the environment, or how subject they are to the dictates of materialism and consumerism, or how they, through the omnipresence of television and advertising, promote uniformity and banality instead of a respect for human uniqueness."

The deterioration of our humanity is no small concern. We are, as the philosopher Pierre Teilhard de Chardin once noted, "spiritual beings having a human experience," not consumers having a material experience. Our souls need time to think, dream, and reflect. We benefit from doing nothing, from going out to play, from giving from the heart and spending time in nature. Most of all we benefit from having healthy, strong, and loving relationships with other people and from exercising the altruistic parts of ourselves. These activities nurture our souls in both hidden and obvious ways.

❖

Once upon a time it was said that all work and no play made Jack a dull boy. Then Jack entered the rat race and became conspicuously industrious. He would probably like to put on his jacket and tell Mom that he's going outside to do nothing. But oops! That's his beeper going off. Gotta go. Might be the boss.

Two Friends, Two Scripts

SCRIPT ONE

Shh! Two friends are in a fitting room trying on clothes.

"So, how do I look?"

"Fabulous."

"Should I buy it?"

"Definitely."

"But it costs a fortune."

"Who cares? Just put it on your credit card."

"Should I *really?* My closet is full of things I haven't worn."

"But this is *your* color! You look so thin."

"I do! You're right. I'll go ahead and charge it. I'll never notice this little bit of extra interest anyway!"

SCRIPT TWO

Shh! Two friends are in a fitting room trying on clothes.

"So, how do I look?"
"Fabulous."
"Should I buy it?"
"Do you need it?"
"No, not really. But I *like* it."
"Can you afford it?"
"Well, no. But I can put it on my credit card."
"Why dig yourself deeper into debt? Your closet is already stuffed with things you've hardly worn."
"That's true. You know, you're right."

"Let's get together for coffee tomorrow and clean out your closet. We can make up a box of clothes for charity. There's a group in our neighborhood that collects clothes for women who are interviewing to get better jobs."

"Good thinking. Thanks, girlfriend!"

Try It, You'll Like It

There was a man in France who went to a lavish dinner party. His hostess had laid forth a beautiful table full of splendid dishes, but for reasons he could not explain, the man wasn't hungry.

"Try something!" his wife whispered when they sat down to table. "You have to eat or the hostess will be insulted."

Listening to his wife, as he always did, the man served himself a small portion and began to eat slowly. It was so delicious, that in short order, he began eating with gusto and even returned for a second helping.

"You know the old saying," his wife remarked later when they had left the party. "It's true–'with the eating comes the appetite.'"

This is a fact of life and most of us know it–our appetites have a mind of their own. There are times when we aren't hungry or thirsty or sleepy or wanting. But then suddenly our appetite is awakened; putting us in touch with desires we didn't know existed within us.

Maybe God understood this back in paradise. When Adam and Eve were wandering in the garden of earthly delights, God warned them not to eat the fruit of the forbidden tree. Perhaps the Almighty knew how easy it is for the serpent of temptation to arouse our ravenous appetites. Perhaps God was trying to spare the first couple from dealing with desires more powerful than they could handle.

Well, as everybody knows, Adam and Eve didn't listen. God's instructions were ignored and they were cast out of the garden, forced to go out into the world. There, they toiled and suffered. Instead of living for all eternity, they grew old and died.

Yet, despite it all, they may have been better off in some respects than people today. Back when the world was new, the forces of temptation were fewer and simpler. There were no television commercials trying to make people feel inadequate because they didn't own a sport-utility vehicle. Or focus groups figuring out how to get children to eat more sugar-coated breakfast cereal. Or marketing gurus inventing ways to get people in search of genuine love and self-esteem to buy jewelry and designer clothes instead. Or infomercials and shopping channels turning yearnings into purchases. Back in the garden, subliminal persuasion wasn't yet a science; and pop-up ads weren't pressuring people to buy, buy, buy on the Internet.

> *What follows from this right of multiplication of desires? In the rich, isolation and spiritual suicide; in the poor, envy and murder.*
>
> —FYODOR DOSTOYEVSKY

In contrast to earlier times, modern society is a complex place. Rife with commercial pressures, it thrives by getting us to purchase what we don't need; want what we can't afford; and pay with interest at the end of the month. There isn't just one serpent urging us to take a bite of the apple. In today's world, a marketing machine with deep-corporate pockets and media savvy is working tirelessly to get us to live beyond our means, to run just to hold our ground, and join the rat race. Dispersing credit cards like Halloween candy, this marketing machine is out to convert the public's fears, hopes, and dreams into cash.

Partners in crime with the marketers are the Merchants of Discontent–the advertisers. This group distinguishes itself by mastering a new art: "the art of making things true by saying they are so," as historian Daniel Boorstin so aptly says. Like fishermen dangling bait over a pool of hungry fish, the advertisers lure the public and attempt to keep them in a state of perpetual dissatisfaction with what they currently have.

The advertisers don't really care if the needs they are filling are real or manufactured, or if the products they pitch are long lasting. As a matter of fact, the more ephemeral the better. "Psychological obsolescence is the double barreled strategy of (1) making the public style-conscious, and then (2) switching styles," writes Vance Packard in *The Hidden Persuaders*.

That said, none of us is a victim. Each of us bears responsibility for our actions and can take steps to resist the onslaught of marketing pressures. We can begin by tuning out the media that feeds our heads with try-it-you'll-like-it messages and make sure that our children are shielded as well. We can take time to differentiate what we want from what we need, and make a "declaration of enough" when we have had our fair share. We can refuse to become slaves to fashion and stop shopping as a leisure sport. We can turn our backs on advertisers who tell us that self-respect, love, or self-confidence come in a gift box. And we can remember the words of Benjamin Franklin who wrote, "'Tis easier to suppress the first Desire than to satisfy all that follows it."

Finally, we must redefine the notion of progress so that it has less to do with what size car or house we own, and more to do with how big our hearts and souls are. We can begin teaching our children that love, caring, and kindness are what really matter so that they don't live with a constant gnawing for an endless stream of material possessions.

Here's another version of the story about a man who attended a dinner party in France. His hostess had laid forth a beautiful table full of many splendid dishes, but for reasons the man could not explain, he wasn't a bit hungry.

"Try something," his wife whispered when they sat down to eat. "You have to eat or the hostess will be insulted."

"No," said the man. "I apologize but I have no appetite this evening. I hope you will allow me to sit in the garden until the others are finished eating."

And so it happened that the man entered the garden. And there he stayed.

What Mice Really Need, Rats Can't Provide

Mice are nice. Go to any kindergarten class and you may see a tank of these warm and furry creatures making their nests, licking their babies, shredding paper, eating seeds, and scampering around playfully. Peaceful and industrious, mice work, eat, and play together contentedly before piling up to rest in a cuddly snowball of white fur.

Rats are not nice. Dirty and threatening, they eat garbage and carry germs. Lurking in dark corners of sewers, drainpipes, and other dank places, these itchy, scratchy creatures of the night have fang-like teeth, spiky tails, and oily backs that make human skin crawl. Rarely does anyone keep a rat as a pet. Unlike mice, rats are not nice.

Why, then, do so many of us act like rats? Why, when gentleness would bring unity, do we choose aggression? Why, when fellowship would bring peace, do we divide and conquer? Fretting over "Who moved *my* cheese?" we forget to make sure whether or not there is enough cheese to go around.

The next time you yearn for peace, togetherness, and a warm snuggle, take a peek inside a tank of mice. See how our furry little friends do it. And remember these few essential rules for mice:

1. No fighting, no biting
2. Be soft, stay clean
3. You scratch my back, I'll scratch yours
4. If you can't fight 'em, lick 'em.
5. Practice random acts of nesting

And remember—what mice really need, rats can't provide.

Redefining Progress

"We made progress," said the economist. "The gross domestic product increased last month by one percent."

"We have work to do," said the social worker. "A child went to bed hungry last night."

❖

"We made progress," said the budget analyst. "Consumer spending rose last week by one percent."

"We have work to do," said the humanitarian. "A homeless family has no place to live."

❖

"We made progress," said the stock analyst. "The market index rose by five percent."

"We have work to do," said the spiritual counselor. "A sick woman can't afford healthcare."

❖

"We made progress," said the market specialist. "Housing starts rose last month by one percent."

"We have work to do," said the rabbi. "An elderly man lives alone and is afraid."

❖

"We made progress," said the pharmaceutical executive. "We've developed a breakthrough drug."

"We have work to do," said the doctor. "These drugs are unaffordable."

"We made progress," said the statistician. "Unemployment is down."

"We have work to do," said the child welfare agent. "Broken homes are on the rise."

❖

We've made progress," said the military strategist. "The missile defense system has been approved."

"We have work to do," said the peace activist. "People everywhere hate us, and hate is the greatest weapon of mass destruction."

❖

Isn't it time we redefined progress? Isn't there work to do?

Part II
Virtue As
Its Own Reward

Doing It Just Because

When I was in fifth grade, a girl in my math class cheated on an exam. I remember feeling sick to my stomach as I watched our teacher haul the girl off to the principal's office. Like a sadistic crowd at the Roman circus, some of my classmates threw spitballs at the girl as she left the class, embarrassed and ashamed by her wrongful act.

That night, I asked my mother why it was wrong to cheat.

"Because," she said, without missing a beat.

"Because?" I echoed back. But that was it. Nothing more was said.

Being ten years old at the time, I wondered if this was the same as "because I said so"—a roadblock answer parents give when they are short-tempered and want to prove that they have the power. My instincts told me this was different. But I didn't know why.

Years later that brief exchange with Mother came back to me when I was raising my own children. Needing to find a rationale that I could offer my daughter and son to be good, upright, and kind people made me examine how religions and societies promote decency, fairness, honesty, and kindness. Since the beginning of time, I discovered, the "reward mentality" has been the dominant reason people have relied on to promote doing the right thing.

Many religions, for example, promise "eternal life inside the pearly gates" in exchange for good conduct on earth. Accumulating celestial bonus points in what might be called a spiritual layaway plan makes heaven the great dividend for walking the straight and narrow before we die. Conversely, the threat of hell, fire, and brimstone aims to deter potential sinners from going astray as part of a spiritual restraining order.

The so-called golden rule is also about rewards. Admonishing us to "Do unto others as you would have them do unto you," the golden rule is less about the hereafter than it is an insurance policy for getting good treatment in the here-and-now. Ignoring the fact that others may not want or need what we want for ourselves, the rule is a philosophical relative of the idea that what-goes-around-comes-around. Motivated by self-interest, we ought to watch what we do.

But as I reviewed those schools of thought, I didn't think my mom's answer—"because"—fell into any of the categories. The more I considered the matter the more I realized that her view centered on the idea that *being good is an end in itself.* It is its own reason and needs no reason, all at once. It didn't matter if there was a heaven or a hell awaiting saints and sinners—though she had been taught by her strict Catholic faith to believe there was both. What matters always is embracing good thoughts, words, and deeds *for their own sake.*

The more I pondered this idea, the more it intrigued me. In a time when so many people are searching for meaning, purpose, and direction in their lives, "doing it because" provides a simple moral compass to guide us through some of the treacheries and detours of the modern world. Doing it because acknowledges that there are moral absolutes that are above explanation and beyond challenge. They are truths that we hold to be self-evident, just like life, liberty, and the pursuit of happiness. Nobody needs to explain why every man, woman, and child on the face of the earth is entitled to them.

What is right, kind, proper, and just, is right, kind, proper, and just. Just *because.*

Machiavelli Got It Wrong

Five hundred years ago, in the time of the great Renaissance, an Italian statesman named Niccolo Machiavelli wrote a book called *The Prince,* which suggested that a leader could use any means necessary—including cruelty, torture, deception, and ruthlessness—to gain and keep power. Launching the idea that the ends justify the means, Machiavelli unleashed a plague of political pollution on the world that not only sanctioned corruption in high places, but also placed too much importance on the results that are produced by actions.

And since then, our world has been focused on getting results.

Look around. Business school instructors, bankers, politicians, and economists all emphasize the need to be results oriented. The reward mentality—bonus points, high yield, and dividends—are paramount in outcome-oriented financial circles. Good results are the goal. Good results get rewarded.

Now, just to be clear about rewards, they do have a place in life. There's nothing wrong with rewarding good deeds, excellent performance, and high standards. Wanting to be recognized for our accomplishments is a part of human nature. If the reward mentality stirs up trouble, it happens when people come to *expect* rewards, when they decide that the reason to act is because they will be rewarded, when right action is abandoned because it hasn't produced the desired rewards.

Imagine life on earth has ended. We die and discover that we are going to heaven because we've been good.

Most of us would undoubtedly like to wind up in heaven if there is such a place. But what if there is no heaven? Should we feel duped? Were we foolish for being honest, truthful, and good? Of course not. We should be virtuous for its own sake. Because it is the right thing to do! Not because of the possible rewards.

To Thine Own Self
Be True

Way back in kindergarten, many of us learned to play
Follow the Leader. You remember the game—one child
parading around the room doing somersaults, twirling,
and jumping up and down, followed by a line of other
children trying to mimic the leader's movements. The
sillier the movements became, the better the spectacle.
That was the whole point. In no time, most of the children were laughing uproariously and look-
ing ridiculous.

As life unfolded, those children grew up.
Some of them became leaders, but most
became followers, taking directions from the
person in front of them. They fell in line and

reacted. They looked to the person ahead of them for cues. Sometimes they looked pretty ridiculous.

So, then, who are you? A leader or a follower? The person who acts or reacts? When you left the playground, did you take charge of your soul?

When we go out into the world, we play a definite role. The world expects it. Either we give orders or take them, as leader or follower.

If someone out in the world gives an order to do a somersault, what will you do?

If someone tells you to jump up and down, will you jump up and down?

If someone tells you to stand on your head, what will you do?

If someone tells you to cheat a little on your taxes, will you cheat a little?

If someone tells you to doctor your time sheet, will you do it?

If someone tells you to run the rat race, will you run the rat race?

If someone tells you that you need to own a gold watch to feel good about yourself, will you go right out and buy one?

If someone tells you to pick out the Jews, what will you do?

Doing what is good, right, moral, and proper means staying your own course, leading not following, acting not reacting. Marching to the beat of your own drummer. And remaining true to your self.

Lead the line. Don't get in line. Or you may feel ridiculous—or worse.

In Idealism Is the Preservation of the World

You see things and you say, "Why?" But I dream things that never were and I say, "Why not?"

—GEORGE BERNARD SHAW

Reiterated and impressed on our hearts by Robert F. Kennedy, these famous words have come to signify a belief that we can attain the impossible. Visionaries, dreamers, geniuses, and perfectionists have always had an allergy for limits. They dream and ask, why not? They take us places that can't be reached and move the world. They do it *because.* Because they are driven by a rare intensity of the soul that pushes them forward.

As we travel through life, there will be people who try to drag us down with their sure sense of what can't be done. They criticize our wishful thinking, calling it pie in the sky. Reject their advances. Don't let them get too close.

When a person routinely says, "Why bother?" calls us Pollyanna, and says, "Go sell your crazy ideas somewhere else," reject their advances. Don't let them into your head. Make it a habit to reject any pattern of thought that is rooted in negativity. Bear in mind that what we think we will become. Think big. Dream big,

That's what Martin Luther King, Jr. did. With his immortal words, "I have a dream," he used hope and inspiration to convey his belief that difficulties of historic proportions could be overcome. His message of optimism about racial harmony survived an assassin's bullet. So does the truth. Since Martin Luther King's death there

has been progress that few—besides himself—ever dreamed
was possible.

One of the few who shared his dreams is the African
leader and Nobel Peace Prize winner Nelson Mandela.
Sounding a trumpet for truth and freedom,
Mandela spent more than twenty years in prison
as punishment for his opposition to apartheid.
At his trial, before his imprisonment, he said,
"I have fought against white domination, and I
have fought against black domination," he said.
"I have cherished the ideal of a democratic and
free society in which all persons will live together in harmony and with equal opportunities. It is an ideal which
I hope to live for and achieve. But, if need be, it is an
ideal for which I am prepared to die."

Here's a challenge to consider. When you look out
on the world tomorrow, try looking through the eyes of

Robert Kennedy and Martin Luther King and Nelson Mandela. See from the perspective of these rabid idealists who fought to preserve the world from the tyranny of what is merely possible. Consider what the world would be like if we all had a dream and asked, "why not?"

Part III
A Change of Heart

Attitude Is Everything

Once upon a time in ancient Greece, the gods decided to punish a man by forcing him to roll a great boulder up a hill. Every time the man got close to the top, near the point of resting, the boulder rolled back down the hill and the man had to start all over. This was the man's fate for all eternity. Not very much fun, to say the least!

The story of this tortured man, whose name was Sisyphus, caught the attention of the French philosopher Albert Camus. Discouraged by the suffering of modern life, Camus believed that the myth of Sisyphus said it all. Having lived through two world wars and great devastation, Camus found much spiritual emptiness all around him. Suffering and struggling—as were the lot in life of Sisyphus—were the only things Camus felt man could really count on.

There is incredible suffering all around us. It can't be denied. And it comes in a wide variety. There are big forms of suffering such as poverty, war, natural disaster, hunger, and random acts of violence. There is also garden-variety suffering that occurs every day in small situations and in familiar ways—people hurting their neighbors, betraying their friends, acting out of jealousy and destructive tendencies towards members of their families.

Given how devastating and commonplace suffering is, it's easy to understand why people get discouraged with life and human nature. Some get so down they question the existence of God rather than exploring what can actually be done to counter their problems.

Perhaps the single greatest thing we can do is to control our attitude. A situation can defeat us, or we can defeat ourselves by getting discouraged. We can see our problems as opportunities that allow us to learn and to grow, or we can decide that any situation, even a minor one, is hopeless—and it most surely will be. We choose to think what we want to think.

Why not counter negativity with a positive attitude?

What do you have to lose? Practicing spiritual defiance creates an opportunity to discover what's possible. Why get discouraged and pessimistic and invite paralysis? In our heart of hearts, we know better than this. Our spirit tells us so. Our intuition tells us so. And so does real life.

Recently, on the news, the presenter told the story of an elderly woman who was driving her car in the Midwest on a rainy night when her vehicle flipped over and sank in a nearby lake, leaving her suspended upside down. As the car gradually filled with water, she was determined not to succumb to a bleak situation and, in a seemingly futile effort, craned her neck to find a pocket of air where she could tuck her nose. Clinging to dear life, the elderly woman hung upside down for forty-eight hours, refusing to give up, believing that she only needed to hold on until the rescue squad arrived. When the emergency workers reached her, they said it was a miracle. God had intervened and spared her life. And He may well have. But the woman had sprinkled her own magic on the situation. She never gave up.

A more familiar story of positive attitude is the saga of Senator John McCain of Arizona who was held prisoner and tortured by the Viet Cong for several years under horrible conditions. Senator McCain held on. In his heart and in his mind, he refused to give up.

Instead of pondering *why* we suffer, our time may be better spent working to alleviate the suffering all around us. That is supported by adopting a positive attitude, where we take responsibility for our experiences. We can debate things into the ground. Or we can make sure our spirits stay intact!

Nurturing a positive attitude can take time. For those with a tendency to see the cup half empty, it is best to begin by listening to what is actually going on inside your head. When a problem looms, do you begin by making a list of all the insurmountable obstacles? Do you get caught up in a cycle of fretting, fear, and worry that creates a whirlpool of pessimism? Nearly every storm cloud has a silver lining. Look for it and go from there.

Optimism is contagious. Whenever possible, surround yourself with creative problem solvers. People who look on the bright side, who see problems as opportunities, often give us the stamina and conviction to go forward.

Last, but not least, say a prayer to whatever higher power you believe in. Put your questions, concerns, and worries out, and ask for help. You never know who might be listening.

Forgiveness as a Path to Wholeness

"I'll never forgive that creep," the young woman wailed. "Not in a million years. One minute he tells me I'm the only one he'll ever love and then the next day I catch him with lipstick on his collar. Have you ever heard of anything so outrageous?"

Maybe not. But it doesn't matter. It doesn't matter what harm has been done to you. It doesn't matter if you have been wounded by the most unreasonable, unkind, self-centered, mean-spirited person on the face of the earth. It doesn't matter if you never harmed a flea, were voted the "world's most innocent victim" and are now being considered for sainthood. Nothing matters but that you forgive.

Forgiveness. Nearly every major religion on earth emphasizes it. Why? What is it about forgiveness that makes it so central to human life?

There are several answers, but perhaps the simplest is that forgiveness sets us free. It unshackles us from an emotional prison that can take a deadly toll on our soul.

As spiritual beings having a human experience, each of us has an obligation to live and grow. That requires being able to soak up all that we can of what is going on now. The gift of awareness helps us to discover who we really are. That's why people spend years training their minds to be still.

When we are stuck in the past, in our thoughts and memories—hostage to anger, resentment, heartache, emotional upheaval, depression, devastation, and misfortune—we are not fully present to the opportunities life holds out to us each day. Releasing us from the past, forgiveness can make us whole by helping us to shed the feeling of victimhood that makes it more difficult to show mercy.

Seeking vengeance when we have been wounded—an eye for an eye—often leads to mass blindness. As Jesus implored, forgive seventy times seven—and even then carry on. Forgive always and often. For surely, forgiveness is the path to wholeness and peace.

Hate: The Most Dangerous Weapon of Mass Destruction

The votes are in, the tally completed. According to language experts polled by CNN, the words "weapons of mass destruction" ranked as Phrase of the Year in 2002, making it the most widely broadcast or printed expression in the English language. Edging out such contenders as "Reality TV," "rogue nations," and "axis of evil," the phrase "weapons of mass destruction" aced first place.

Not surprising. Since 9/11, with elevated security concerns around the world, there has been a surge in media reports about chemical, biological, and nuclear weapons. Chilling stories of nerve agents, smallpox, mustard gas, anthrax, and warheads—among other deadly threats—

have dominated the news. As Dorothy said when she arrived in Oz, "We're not in Kansas any more."

Where we are is in a grave new world of fear and uncertainty, a place of security alerts and safe rooms designed to ward off weapons of mass destruction. Whoops! There's that phrase again, conjuring up the dark possibilities of things to come.

And that's the point. Powerful and evocative, words shape our expectation of what's ahead. Not only do words convey ideas and information. They stoke fear and dread, carry threats and warnings, as well as offer a more positive vision of hope and possibility.

For instance, when Martin Luther King said, "I have a dream," a nation afflicted by racism and segregation rallied to his call for justice and equality. When John F. Kennedy said, "Ask not what your country can do for you, ask what you can do for your country," he inspired a nation to serve. In an earlier time, when FDR presided over a depression-ravaged America, his conviction that "there is nothing to fear but fear itself" instilled courage and purpose in the nation.

Other messages have provoked fear. Psychologists report a steep rise in "ambient anxiety" since the post-9/11 media fixation on terrorism. This free-floating fear that everyday living is fraught with danger has sent many members of the public scurrying to hardware stores to stock up on flashlights, batteries, duct tape, and other emergency supplies.

Now, being prepared for an emergency isn't a bad idea. Every home needs a first-aid kit along with a few candles or flashlights in case the lights go out. Precautionary measures, as every good Boy Scout will avow, make sense. But when fear and worry begin to tint our overall outlook on life, dictating what we think and do, it is time to readjust our perspective. We can call this finding a sense of balance, of realism that is not skewed towards the negative or positive.

This balance comes in several forms. Emotionally, it starts with the decision to root out pessimistic thinking. This deadly frame of mind, which can lead to depression and despair, stems from the tendency to view problems as "permanent and "universal" when they may only be "local and "temporary," according to psychologist Martin Seligman. By eroding hope that a solution can be reached, a pessimistic attitude will ensure that it won't, becoming a self-fulfilling prophecy.

A second strategy is to limit our exposure to negative messages. When the news recycles the same dire reports over and over again, why not change the channel? As First Lady Laura Bush counseled during 9/11, it was pointless and damaging for small children to see airplanes crashing into the World Trade Towers over and over again on television. Why permit impressionable minds to be hypnotized by numbing scenes of death and destruction?

Just as important as tuning out the Destruction Channel is identifying the chronic complainers in our lives. These are the people who talk endlessly about their difficulties, seeming to prefer the futility of their problems over sure-fire solutions. Being constructive isn't on the radar of these Cassandras.

But their eyes can be opened.

Consider this example of a recent dinner party among friends. After the plates were cleared and the talk turned to world affairs, one gentleman declared that catastrophe was inevitable now that outlaw nations possessed weapons of mass destruction. "Sooner or later we are all going to be blown to bits," this purveyor of doom and gloom casually predicted.

"Well," offered another guest, "let's apply some 'lessons of mass compassion' and 'weapons of vast affection' to ensure that peace prevails. After all, hate is the greatest weapon of mass destruction."

Caught off guard by the wordplay, the table fell silent. When the conversation resumed a short time later, the mood was changed. Instead of swapping tips on the best way to seal their windows with duct tape, ideas were traded about using the spiritual flashlights of kindness, tolerance, and love to light up our troubled world. "Just because terrorism is a grave problem," one guest said, "doesn't mean we can't heal our personal rifts."

Pie in the sky? Some might say so. But by the end of the night there were no disbelievers around that particular table. Only new converts to the idea that love, creativity, and optimism can make a real difference and, perhaps, even conquer all. And who knows—maybe the next time the group gathers for dinner the Phrase of the Year will be something like, "Help Proliferate Love."

And why not? Martin Luther King isn't the only one who can dream.

From the "Me Generation" to the "We Generation"

To get out of the rat race, the pundits tell us, we must simplify our lives. Clean out our closets, be frugal with our pennies, and adopt an "attitude of gratitude." Slow down, seek quiet, and always remember that less is more.

It's good advice for many of us. But we also have to open our eyes to the fact that not everyone is as fortunate as we are. In fact the divide between the haves and have-nots, in our own country and throughout the world, is actually growing larger. We may need to simplify but when you're hungry, poor, or homeless, less isn't more.

For those people, less is . . . less! For some people, simplifying isn't an option. It's a sign of luxury!

There are two distinct groups in today's world—the haves and the have-nots. The have's possess money, privilege, creature comforts, and lots of options. The extent to which their lives are frantic is often a matter of the choices they make. By taking control and making better decisions, the haves can improve their quality of life. Not so for the have-nots. Lacking resources, opportunities, education, and power, they struggle to make ends meet.

As a society, we have choices to make. We can leave the disenfranchised to pull themselves up and out of despair by their own bootstraps. Or we can heed the words of Mahatma Gandhi who said, "Recall the face of the poorest and the most helpless man whom you may have seen and ask yourself, if the step you contemplate is going to be of any use to *him*. Will he be able to gain anything by it? Will it restore him to a control over his own life and destiny?"

In the 1980s, Tom Wolfe coined the phrase the "Me Generation" to describe the self-indulgent, egocentric lifestyle so many of us chose to live. The Me Generation spends amply and wastes lavishly, often taking pride in overdoing it. The Me Generation focuses on I, me, mine, pausing only to say, "Enough about me. What do *you* think about me?"

Perhaps it is time to ask whether we can afford this behavior anymore. In a world where many eat like pigs but many more go hungry; in a world where millions have everything they desire but many still have holes in their hearts from sorrow, alienation, and suffering—can we afford the inequity? Can we turn a blind eye to the desperation all around us?

The writer Ayn Rand once noted in an interview that "man is not a sacrificial animal, that he has the right to exist for his own sake, neither sacrificing himself to others, nor others to himself." There is truth in this statement. But a balance needs to be struck between self-sacrifice and the common good. "Furthering the common good does not require that we forego self-interest, but rather that we are able to see our own interests linked to those of others," as Frances Moore Lappe commented in *Rediscovering America's Values*. "It requires a society that enables citizens to express the very human need to act on our deepest values as well as on our private interests."

This means finding where the interests of the individual and the group overlap. Perhaps it means asking: Isn't it time to move from the Me Generation to the We Generation? To reach for the common good? To put more effort into service and sacrifice? To remember the words of the Roman Pliny the Elder who once wrote, "For mortal to aid mortal—this is god." To take to heart the words of Virginia Woolf who once said, "One of the signs of passing youth is the birth of a sense of fellowship with other human beings as we take our place among them."

It doesn't take much. Everybody has something to offer and small gestures mean a lot. You can begin to reach across the divide by taking your hand out of your own pocket and using it to lift someone else up. It isn't only about writing a check. Money is one way to help. We can also give our time, love, and attention. Mentor a child. Visit the sick. Bring a hot meal to a hungry family. Offer counsel, support, a listening ear. Share our surplus of clothes or our knowledge of how to get out from under. Every little bit counts.

Perhaps the goal is best put by the early twentieth-century French critic Charles du Bois who once wrote that "the important thing is this: to be able at any moment to sacrifice what we are for what we could become." Lest we forget that to those whom much is given, much is required.

Welcome to the We Generation.

God Is Watching—
Look Busy!

A popular television show called *Candid Camera*, which aired in the 1960s and 1970s, used hidden cameras to catch unsuspecting people in the act of being themselves. These unwitting participants were usually put in odd situations and forced to make choices that were captured on film for the delight of the viewers at home.

Choices. In the final analysis, that is what life is about. The issue may be as trivial as where to park our car or as weighty as whether to adopt a child. Will we tell the truth or lie? Yield or hold our ground? What will we do?

We may think that these choices affect us alone, or the people in our lives. But as the popular T-shirt says, *God is watching—look busy!*

Everything we do on earth is between us and God. Just as God is our judge, He is also our witness. He knows all, sees all, and is never far away. That being true, here's the question: When God looks at us, what do we want Him to see? A person who seeks justice, practices kindness, and walks humbly on the earth? A righteous person who gives to the poor and helps the homeless and the sick? A person who leaves each situation better than he or she found it? A person who is merciful and gentle, loyal and honorable, who lives the doctrine of unconditional love?

Or do we want Him to see a short-tempered individual who lashes out when people anger us? Who is selfish and self-centered, accusatory and manipulative, controlling and jealous, proud and contemptuous of others, who is boastful, arrogant, and vindictive?

How would we like to be viewed?

Imagine each day, as you walk through your life, that God is in the corner with a hidden camera. The film is always rolling and your behavior is going to be shown to the nation in prime time. Everything you have done will be available for all to see because God plans to show it unedited. You will be caught in the act of being yourself. This is your show. You are the star. What part do you want to play? Hero or villain? Saint or sinner? In the final analysis, it's up to you.

Part IV
Your Turn

Creating a Life
That Counts

She was a little girl, barely three feet tall and only seven years old. But everywhere she went she was asked the same question.

"What do you want to be when you grow up?" her teacher would ask.

"What do you want to be when you grow up?" her camp counselor would inquire.

"What do you want to be when you grow up?" her minister would query.

And the girl always fell quiet, not sure quite what to say.

One day, when her aunt came for a visit, the woman pressed the child as none had done before.

"You are seven years old now," her aunt said in a booming voice that made the girl tremble. "Do you know what you want to be when you grow up?"

As usual, the girl fell silent. But her aunt kept pressing.

"Would you like to be a writer like your father or an accountant like your mother? Or perhaps you would like to be a nurse like me."

The girl fell quiet again but this time something inside of her was stirring. She paused and reflected for a few seconds before deciding to speak.

"I have given some thought to your question, Auntie," the girl finally answered in a voice that rang with conviction. "When I grow up, I think I'll be myself."

Turning our backs on the expectations of the world can take a special kind of courage. That courage is available to each of us but we have to know where to look for it, as the actress Shirley MacLaine suggested during an appearance on *The Phil Donahue Show* in the 1980s. When Ms. MacLaine was asked where she went for strength and advice, her answer was simple:

"Inside," she said.

The interior landscape of our soul is a rich place full of hidden resources. When we are fearful, searching, or confused, enlightenment or insight can often be found by turning away from the noise and the haste of modern life. So, here is a modest proposal. Every so often, go inside. Take time out of your hectic day and be quiet. Just for a few minutes. Find a quiet corner away from the rat race. Be still and consider what is missing from your life. Or what you have but have forgotten to appreciate. Ask for directions that will lead you to a life of deeper meaning and purpose—a life that counts. Then, when you have asked your questions, listen. Think about the story of this little girl, just seven years old, who stood up for herself against the powers of the world. She answered for herself with firm conviction. And so can you.

Find time. Make time. Because your life and the quality of life in the world depends on it.

Making Your Own
"Declaration of Enough"

In the space allocated below and on the next page, take the opportunity to jot down your thoughts about areas of your life where you would like to make a change. It could be a change in the way you spend your time, money, effort, or energy. Are you ready to make what simplicity advocates like to call a Declaration of Enough? In the end, it's up to you.

Write it down and set the wheels of change in motion! Your first draft need not be more than a few paragraphs. That's enough to start moving in the right direction.

Otherworldly Possessions

"I hereby bequeath all my worldly possessions to . . ."

It's a familiar line from a typical will. Final testimonies often carry this phrase. When somebody dies, spelling out how their cash, land, possessions, and investments will be divided is a common practice.

But wait a minute. Who says an inheritance has to be either money or property? Isn't there more to leave to our loved ones than cash and land, houses and stocks, apartments and insurance policies? A growing number of people are saying, "Yes." They want to discuss their otherworldly assets, the riches of the spirit, the intangibles they have gathered during their time on earth. When they sit down to divvy up their possessions, they are writing ethical wills or living legacies that go much deeper. Avoiding all mention of our material assets, these testimonials spell out our non-material wealth and blessings—the spiritual lessons, values, experiences, and truths we have gathered during out lives.

On July 7, 2004, the *Christian Science Monitor* reported, "many cultures have precedents for handing down advice and blessings to younger generations. In 1050, for example, a Jewish father wrote a letter for his son to read after he died, extolling the importance of a debt-free life." The newspaper goes on to report that a Minneapolis-based doctor named Barry Baines established a Web site about ethical wills after meeting a patient "who felt he had nothing to pass on to his family because he hadn't been materially successful." Dr. Baines and his chaplain helped him write an ethical will, and "his spiritual suffering disappeared," described Baines, who is quoted in the *Monitor.*

No formulas dictate what an ethical will should contain or in what language it ought to be written. It is a highly personal document that springs from the heart and soul of its author. While some legacies are put on paper, others are recorded on video. The technology matters less than capturing the sentiment.

So then, what do you have to bequeath? Your passion for family life? Your dedication to the truth? Your appreciation of humility? Your belief that laughter is the best medicine? A recognition that we ought to forgive and forget? Your experience that time heals all wounds, and an appreciation of the importance of developing patience?

Share the legacy of what has mattered most in your life so that those your loved ones can benefit from your insights. Look yourself in the heart and record the greatest truths you see there. Remember, your life experience counts. Why not give the greatest gift of all to the people you love the most?

Use this space to record your ethical will:

I WOULD LIKE TO LEAVE THESE LESSONS, TRUTHS, EXPERIENCES AND BLESSINGS TO MY HEIRS . . .

Five Questions Worth Asking

1. Are you looking for direction?

You have to trust your inner knowing. If you have a clear mind and an open heart, you won't have to search for direction. Direction will come to you.

—PHIL JACKSON AND HUGH DELEHANTY
IN *SACRED HOOPS*

2. Are you ready to emancipate yourself?

Our discontent begins by finding false villains whom we can accuse of deceiving us. Next we find false heroes whom we expect to liberate us. The hardest, most discomforting discovery is that each of us must emancipate himself.

> —DANIEL BOORSTIN IN *THE IMAGE*

3. What are you willing to sacrifice?

The important thing is this: to be able at any moment to sacrifice what we are for what we could become.

> —CHARLES DU BOIS IN *APPROXIMATIONS*

4. Are you strong enough to look in the mirror?

Whoever looks in the mirror of the water will see first of all his own face. Whoever goes to himself risks a confrontation with himself . . . This confrontation is the first test of courage on the inner way, a test sufficient to frighten off most people.

> —CARL JUNG

5. Do you know when to speak and when to be quiet?

I am very little inclined on any occasion to say any-thing unless I hope to produce some good by it.

—ABRAHAM LINCOLN

It is better to keep your mouth shut and appear stupid than to open it and remove all doubt.

—MARK TWAIN

Resources

Affluenza, the videotape, shown on PBS, and marketed through Bullfrog Films.

Quotationary, written by Leonard Roy Frank and published by Random House. This book is an incredible compendium of provocative ideas and quotes—an important book for every home library!

The Image, written by Daniel Boorstin and published by Vintage Books.

For information on the Voluntary Simplicity Movement, contact Seeds of Simplicity, P.O. Box 9955, Glendale, CA 91226, 818-247-4332; *www.simpleliving.net.*

For information about the Center for a New American Dream, contact: The Center for a New American Dream,

6930 Carroll Ave., Suite 900, Takoma Park, MD 20912, 301-891-3683, www.newdream.org. The center's president, Betsy Taylor, is the author of an inspiring parenting book, *What Kids Really Want That Money Can't Buy*, published by Warner.

For information about Redefining Progress, log on to *www.progress.org.* This group is a nonpartisan, nonprofit organization, based in Oakland, CA, and Washington, DC, and develops policies and tools that "reorient the economy to care for people and nature first."

For information about "simplifying your life, reducing consumption, and learning more about how to adapt environmentally sustainable practices in our homes, workplaces, and communities" contact Vermont Earth Institute, P.O. Box 466, Norwich, VT, 05055, 802-333-3664, *www.vtearthinstitute.org.*

For information about the work of media analyst Kalle Lasne, author of Culture Jam, log onto *www.adbusters.org.*

For information about ethical wills, log on to *www.yourethicalwill.com* or *www.ethicalwill.com.*

About the Author

Joann Davis is a former publishing executive and the author of *The Best Things in Life Aren't Things* and *What I Love Most About You.* She lives with her husband Kenny and two children, Jenny and Colin, in New York City and Dorset, Vermont.

To Our Readers

Conari Press, an imprint of Red Wheel/Weiser, publishes books on topics ranging from spirituality, personal growth, and relationships to women's issues, parenting, and social issues. Our mission is to publish quality books that will make a difference in people's lives—how we feel about ourselves and how we relate to one another. We value integrity, compassion, and receptivity, both in the books we publish and in the way we do business.

Our readers are our most important resource, and we value your input, suggestions, and ideas about what you would like to see published. Please feel free to contact us, to request our latest book catalog, or to be added to our mailing list.

Conari Press
An imprint of Red Wheel/Weiser, LLC
P.O. Box 612
York Beach, ME 03910-0612
www.conari.com

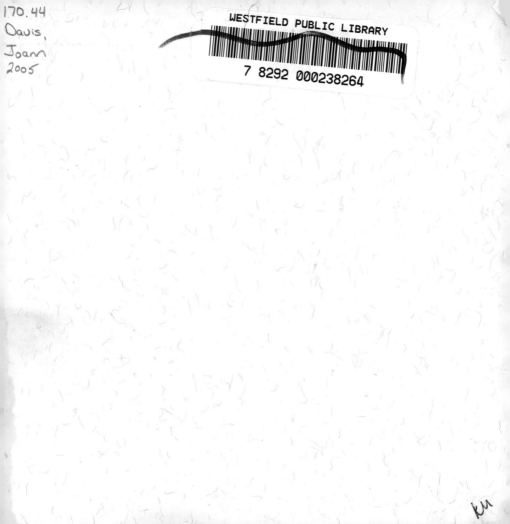

ku